FIRST BIOGRAPHIES

Benjamin Franklin

Cassie Mayer

Heinemann Library
Chicago, Illinois

© 2008 Heinemann Library
a division of Reed Elsevier Inc.
Chicago, Illinois

Customer Service **888-454-2279**

Visit our Web site at **www.heinemannlibrary.com**

Photo research by Tracy Cummins and Tracey Engel
Designed by Kimberly R. Miracle
Maps by Mapping Specialists, Ltd.
Printed and bound in China by South China Printing Company

10 09 08 07
10 9 8 7 6 5 4 3 2 1

10 Digit ISBN: 1-4034-9970-5 (hc)   1-4034-9979-9 (pb)

Library of Congress Cataloging-in-Publication Data
Mayer, Cassie.
  Benjamin Franklin / Cassie Mayer.
    p. cm. -- (First biographies)
  Includes bibliographical references and index.
  ISBN 978-1-4034-9970-7 (hc) -- ISBN 978-1-4034-9979-0 (pb)
  1. Franklin, Benjamin, 1706-1790--Juvenile literature. 2. Statesmen--United States--Biography--Juvenile literature. 3. Scientists--United States--Biography--Juvenile literature. 4. Inventors--United States--Biography--Juvenile literature. 5. Printers--United States--Biography--Juvenile literature. I. Title.
  E302.6.F8M39 2008
  973.3092--dc22
  [B]
                    2007010525

Acknowledgements
The author and publisher are grateful to the following for permission to reproduce copyright material: ©Art Resource **pp. 4** (The Philadelphia Museum of Art), **22** (HIP); ©Corbis **pp. 5** (Bettmann), **9** (Lake County Museum), **10** (Bettmann), **11** (Bettmann), **13** (Bettmann), **18** (Bettmann), **23b** (Lake County Museum); ©The Granger Collection **p. 12**; ©Library of Congress Prints and Photographs Division **p. 20**; ©Mary Evans Picture Library **p. 6**; ©National Archives **p. 17**; ©North Wind Picture Archives **pp. 14**, **21**; ©Picture History **pp. 15, 16.**

Cover image reproduced with permission of ©Art Resource (HIP). Back cover image reproduced with permission of ©Library of Congress Prints and Photographs Division.

Contents

Introduction

Benjamin Franklin was a great leader. He was a Founding Father of the United States.

Founding Fathers helped create the United States. The United States is a country.

Early Life

Franklin was born in 1706.
He was born in Massachusetts.

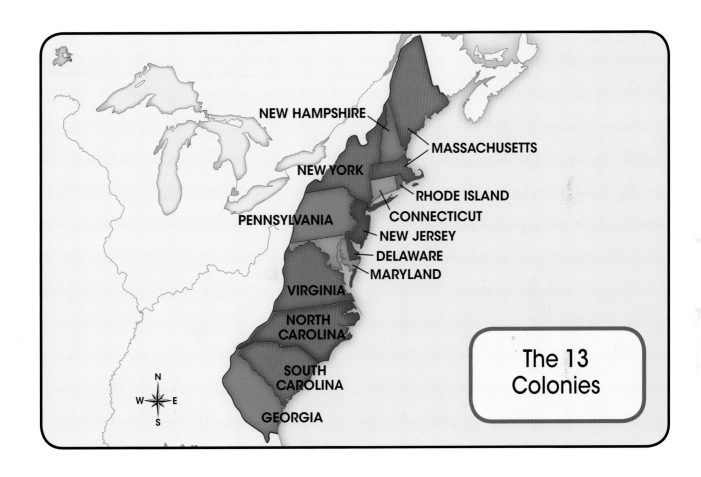

The 13 Colonies

The United States was not a country yet.
It was called the American colonies.

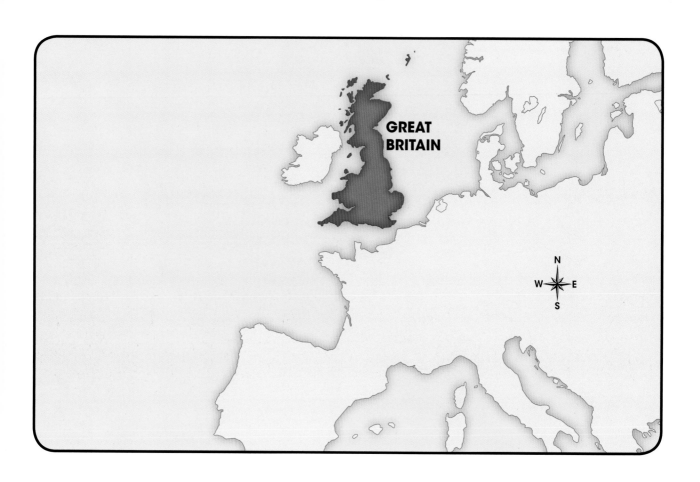

Most of the colonies were led by
Great Britain.

Printer

When Franklin was young, he worked at a print shop.

When Franklin grew up, he made his own newspaper. He wrote for the newspaper.

Scientist

Lightning

Franklin was a great scientist.
He liked to study things in nature.

Inventor

Franklin was a great inventor.
An inventor creates new things.

Bifocals

Franklin invented special glasses.

Founding Father

Franklin wanted to create a new country.
He did not want to be led by Great Britain.

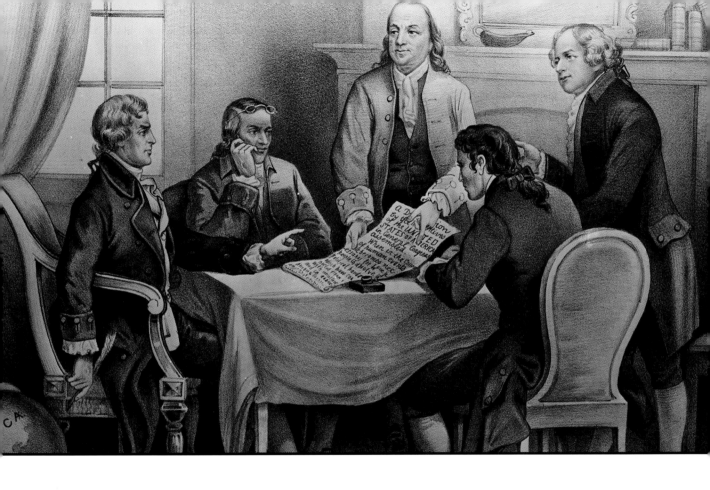

Many leaders agreed with Franklin.
They decided to have a meeting.

Franklin was chosen to go to the meeting.
He helped create a special paper.

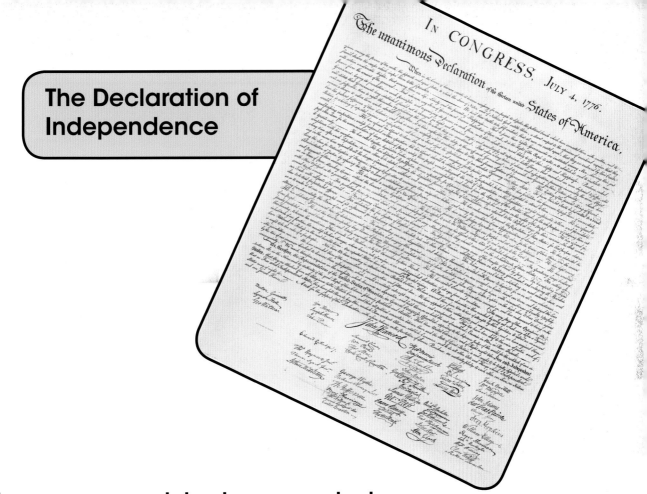

The Declaration of Independence

The paper said why people in the colonies wanted to be free.

Revolutionary War

The people in the colonies went to war with Great Britain. Franklin helped get money for the war.

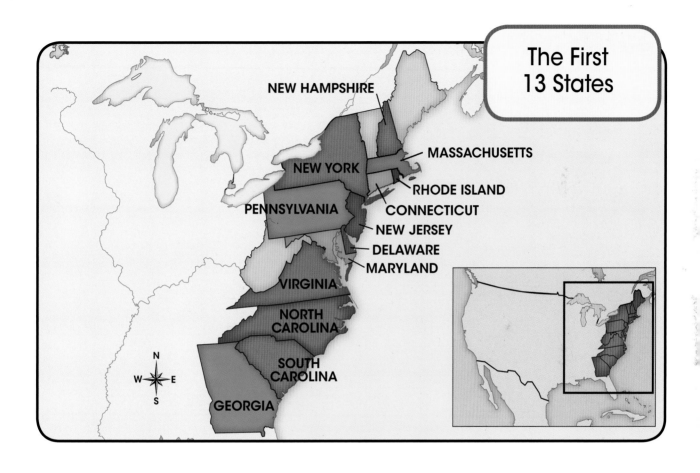

The First 13 States

NEW HAMPSHIRE
MASSACHUSETTS
NEW YORK
RHODE ISLAND
CONNECTICUT
PENNSYLVANIA
NEW JERSEY
DELAWARE
MARYLAND
VIRGINIA
NORTH CAROLINA
SOUTH CAROLINA
GEORGIA

The people in the colonies won the war.
They created the United States of America.

Leader

Franklin became the leader of Pennsylvania in 1785. Pennsylvania is a state.

He helped make rules for the people
in the state.

Why We Remember Him

Franklin was an important American leader. Franklin helped create our country.

Picture Glossary

country an area of land under one leader

print shop a place where books and paper are made

Timeline

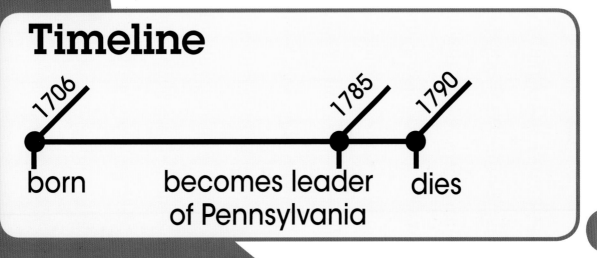

1706 — born

1785 — becomes leader of Pennsylvania

1790 — dies

Index

Note to Parents and Teachers

This series introduces prominent historical figures, focusing on the significant events of each person's life and their impact on American society. Illustrations and primary sources are used to enhance students' understanding of the text.

The text has been carefully chosen with the advice of a literacy expert to enable beginning readers success while reading independently or with moderate support. An expert in the field of early childhood social studies curriculum was consulted to provide interesting and appropriate content.

You can support children's nonfiction literacy skills by helping students use the table of contents, headings, picture glossary, and index.